Love and Laughter

Romantic Comedy

Lily Enchant

Love and Laughter

Romantic Comedy, Volume 1

Lily Enchant

Published by Blissful Romance Books, 2024.

LOVE AND LAUGHTER

First edition. March 31, 2024.

Copyright © 2024 Lily Enchant.

ISBN: 979-8224795123

Written by Lily Enchant.

Also by Lily Enchant

Contemporary Romance
Heartstrings Unraveled

Romantic Comedy
Love and Laughter

Table of Contents

Love and Laughter
Romantic Comedy

Lily Enchant

Chapter 1: Introduction

Sarah Thompson, with her bright eyes and an infectious smile, was known as the life of the party in the small town of Willowbrook. Her quick wit and sharp sense of humor made her the center of attention wherever she went. Whether it was cracking jokes at the local café or finding herself in the most comical predicaments, Sarah had a way of turning every situation into a laugh-out-loud moment.

One sunny morning, Sarah stepped into the bustling café, her favorite spot in town. As she made her way to the counter, she couldn't help but overhear a conversation at the neighboring table. A group of friends was discussing the upcoming comedy festival, the highlight of the town's social calendar.

Eager to join in on the conversation, Sarah approached the table with a mischievous grin. "Did someone say comedy festival? Count me in! I tell you, I've got more jokes up my sleeve than a clown at a circus!"

The group burst into laughter, and a young man with tousled hair and a twinkle in his eyes turned to Sarah. "Well, well, if it isn't the town's resident funny lady. I'm Ethan, by the way. Nice to meet you."

Sarah extended her hand, unable to contain her playful banter. "Ethan, huh? I hope you've got a good sense of humor because my jokes are top-notch."

Ethan chuckled, his eyes sparkling with amusement. "I'm up for the challenge. Let's see if you can keep me laughing."

Sarah and Ethan spent the next hour engaged in a witty back-and-forth, exchanging clever one-liners and humorous anecdotes. Their conversation flowed effortlessly, as if they had known each other for years. Sarah was intrigued by Ethan's quick wit and his ability to match her joke for joke.

As they parted ways, Sarah couldn't help but feel a flutter of excitement. There was something about Ethan that ignited a spark within her, and she couldn't wait to see him again. Little did she know that their paths were destined to cross in even more hilariously unexpected ways, setting the stage for a rom-com adventure unlike any other.

NESTLED IN THE PICTURESQUE countryside, the town of Willowbrook was a hidden gem with its cobblestone streets, colorful storefronts, and a community that exuded warmth and laughter. Known for its offbeat charm, Willowbrook had become a haven for artists, dreamers, and those seeking a respite from the hustle and bustle of city life.

The heart of the town was its annual comedy festival, a beloved tradition that brought together both locals and visitors from afar. The festival was a celebration of laughter and showcased a diverse array of talented comedians from all walks of life. From stand-up performances to improv shows and hilarious skits, the festival was a riotous event that infused the town with an electric energy.

Sarah Thompson strolled along the main street, taking in the sights and sounds of the bustling town. Colorful banners advertising the upcoming comedy festival fluttered in the gentle breeze, drawing her attention. She paused in front of a quirky little bookstore, its shelves overflowing with books of all genres.

Curiosity got the better of her, and Sarah stepped inside, greeted by the comforting scent of old pages and the soft sound of jazz playing in the background. She perused the shelves, running her fingers along the spines, her eyes lighting up with delight as she discovered a hidden gem—a book on practical jokes and humorous anecdotes.

Unbeknownst to Sarah, a fellow book lover stood beside her, also engrossed in the collection of books. The stranger, a bespectacled man with a mischievous glint in his eyes, couldn't help but notice Sarah's infectious enthusiasm.

"Ah, I see you've stumbled upon the humor section," he remarked, a playful smile dancing on his lips.

Sarah turned to face him, her eyes widening with excitement. "Oh, yes! I can't resist a good laugh. Do you have any recommendations?"

The man chuckled, his voice carrying a hint of mischief. "Well, if you're after a good chuckle, you simply must read 'The Jester's Guide to Life.' It's a collection of hilarious anecdotes that will keep you in stitches."

Sarah's laughter echoed through the bookstore as she reached for the book, her eyes meeting the stranger's in a moment of shared mirth. "I like your taste, mister. I'm Sarah, by the way."

He extended his hand, a twinkle in his eyes. "Call me Henry. Nice to meet you, Sarah. Perhaps we can share a few laughs over a cup of coffee?"

And just like that, in the heart of Willowbrook, amidst the laughter and literary delights, Sarah's journey of love and laughter began.

SARAH THOMPSON HAD always been a firm believer in the power of love and laughter. Growing up in a small town, she had witnessed countless romances blossoming amidst the backdrop of whimsical moments and hilarious escapades. Sarah's own heart yearned for a love story that would rival the most captivating tales she had read.

As she sat at her favorite café, sipping her coffee and scrolling through a dating app on her phone, Sarah couldn't help but let out a giggle at the absurdity of some profiles she came across. Her friends often teased her about her knack for finding humor in every situation, but deep down, Sarah longed for a genuine connection and a partner who could match her wit.

Lost in her thoughts, Sarah didn't notice the arrival of her best friend, Lily, until Lily plopped down next to her with a mischievous grin.

"Sarah, my dear, what's got you chuckling to yourself?" Lily asked, raising an eyebrow.

Sarah glanced up, a mischievous glint in her eyes. "Oh, Lily, you won't believe the characters I've encountered on this dating app. It's like a comedy show in itself!"

Lily chuckled and leaned in closer. "Well, my dear, you certainly have a way of attracting interesting personalities. I have no doubt your Mr. Right is out there, waiting to share a lifetime of laughter with you."

Sarah sighed, a mixture of hope and longing in her voice. "I hope so, Lily. I want to find someone who understands my love for laughter and embraces my quirkiness. Someone who can make me laugh until my sides ache."

Lily playfully nudged Sarah's arm. "Don't worry, Sarah. Love has a way of finding us when we least expect it. Just keep being your hilarious self, and the right person will come along."

Sarah smiled, her eyes sparkling with determination. "You're right, Lily. I won't give up on love or laughter. In the meantime, I'll continue to embrace every humorous moment that life throws my way."

Little did Sarah know that her desire for love and her ability to find humor in every situation would soon lead her down a path filled with laughter, unexpected encounters, and a romance that would leave her breathless.

Chapter 2: The Comedy Festival

As the days grew closer to the much-anticipated comedy festival, Sarah found herself fully immersed in the whirlwind of preparations. She had volunteered to help organize the event, eager to be a part of the laughter-filled extravaganza that had brought joy to Willowbrook year after year.

Sarah's first task was to coordinate with the local venues and comedians, ensuring that everything was in place for the festival. Armed with a clipboard and a bright smile, she visited the town's comedy clubs and theaters, engaging in lively conversations with the performers and venue owners.

At one particular comedy club, Sarah found herself in a meeting with the owner, Mr. Jenkins, a seasoned comedian himself. With his graying hair and a twinkle in his eye, Mr. Jenkins exuded the charm and wit that had made him a local legend.

"I must say, Sarah, it's refreshing to have someone as enthusiastic as you helping out with the festival," Mr. Jenkins remarked, leaning back in his chair.

Sarah beamed with pride, her excitement palpable. "Thank you, Mr. Jenkins. I've always been a big fan of comedy, and being a part of this festival is a dream come true. I want to make sure it's the funniest and most memorable event yet!"

Mr. Jenkins chuckled, his laughter filling the room. "Well, my dear, with your passion and knack for finding humor in every situation, I have no doubt that the festival will be a roaring success."

As Sarah and Mr. Jenkins continued their conversation, discussing logistics and brainstorming ideas for the festival, a familiar voice chimed in from the doorway.

"And I have no doubt that Sarah's laughter will light up the stage like no other," said Ethan, the witty young man she had met at the café.

Sarah's heart skipped a beat as she turned to face Ethan, who was grinning from ear to ear. "Ethan! What are you doing here?"

He sauntered into the room, his eyes twinkling with mischief. "I just happened to be passing by and overheard that the comedy festival was in the works. Figured I'd come and offer my assistance, considering I can make you laugh like no one else."

Sarah's cheeks flushed with a mixture of surprise and delight. "Well, you certainly know how to make an entrance, don't you? I'd welcome your help with open arms."

As they all sat around the table, sharing ideas and laughter, Sarah couldn't help but feel a sense of excitement. Little did she know that the comedy festival would not only bring side-splitting hilarity to the town but also set the stage for a series of comical and heartfelt moments that would shape her romantic journey.

AS THE COMEDY FESTIVAL drew nearer, Sarah found herself knee-deep in a flurry of mishaps and comical misunderstandings. It seemed as if the universe had conspired to add an extra dose of laughter to the already humorous event.

One sunny afternoon, Sarah stood in the festival's headquarters, surrounded by stacks of paperwork and a to-do list that seemed to multiply by the minute. She scratched her head, trying to make sense of the jumble of notes and schedules.

Just then, Lily burst through the door, her face flushed with excitement. "Sarah! You won't believe the chaos that's unfolding at the comedy club down the street!"

Sarah's eyes widened, her curiosity piqued. "What happened, Lily? Is everything all right?"

Lily nodded, barely able to contain her laughter. "Well, it seems that there was a mix-up with the performers' schedules. One of the comedians accidentally walked into a yoga class instead of the green room, thinking it was a backstage area. You can imagine the confusion!"

Sarah burst into laughter, picturing the scene in her mind. "Oh, no! I hope they didn't disrupt the class too much!"

Lily chuckled. "Apparently, the comedian tried to incorporate some yoga moves into his routine, thinking it was all part of the act. The yoga instructor was a good sport about it and even joined in on the laughter!"

The two friends giggled uncontrollably, finding humor in the unexpected mishap. As they finally composed themselves, Sarah's phone buzzed with a text message. It was Henry, the bespectacled man she had met at the bookstore.

"Henry wants to meet up to discuss the festival. He mentioned something about a 'top-secret surprise,'" Sarah shared with Lily, a mix of curiosity and excitement in her voice.

Lily raised an eyebrow playfully. "A top-secret surprise? I wonder what he has up his sleeve. Knowing Henry, it's bound to be something delightfully hilarious."

Later that day, Sarah met Henry at a cozy café, their conversation punctuated by laughter and animated gestures. As they discussed the festival, Sarah couldn't help but notice a mischievous glint in Henry's eyes.

"Sarah, my dear, I have a brilliant idea for the festival," Henry exclaimed, his excitement contagious.

Sarah leaned forward, her curiosity piqued. "Do tell, Henry. I'm all ears."

With a grin, Henry revealed his plan, which involved an elaborate prank to be played during one of the comedy performances. Sarah's eyes widened in a mixture of astonishment and amusement.

"You want to do what? That's... that's absolutely outrageous!" Sarah exclaimed between fits of laughter.

Henry chuckled, his eyes sparkling with mischief. "Exactly! It'll be the highlight of the festival, guaranteed to have everyone rolling in the aisles with laughter."

As Sarah and Henry continued to brainstorm and share their love for humorous surprises, they couldn't help but revel in the joy of their shared laughter. Little did they know that their collaboration would not only bring laughter to the festival but also deepen their connection in unexpected ways.

THE DAY OF THE COMEDY festival had finally arrived, and the entire town of Willowbrook buzzed with excitement. The venues were adorned with colorful banners and the air was filled with anticipation. Amongst the sea of eager attendees, Sarah found herself seated near the front row of the main stage, eagerly awaiting the comedic delights that awaited her.

As the spotlight illuminated the stage, a charismatic figure stepped forward, commanding the attention of the audience. It was Ethan Reynolds, a renowned stand-up comedian with an infectious smile and a reputation for leaving audiences in stitches.

Sarah's heart skipped a beat as Ethan launched into his routine, effortlessly weaving tales of everyday mishaps and relatable observations. His comedic timing was impeccable, and his jokes struck a chord with Sarah's own love for laughter.

Beside her, Lily leaned in and whispered, "Sarah, I think you might have found your match made in comedy heaven."

Sarah blushed, her eyes fixed on Ethan as he worked the crowd with ease. "He's incredible, Lily. I can't help but be drawn to his charisma and talent."

After the show, Sarah found herself lingering near the stage, hoping for a chance to speak with Ethan. As luck would have it, their paths crossed near the backstage area, and Sarah mustered up the courage to approach him.

"Ethan, that was an amazing performance. I'm Sarah," she said, her voice tinged with excitement.

Ethan turned towards her, a warm smile gracing his lips. "Nice to meet you, Sarah. I'm glad you enjoyed the show. Your laughter was music to my ears."

Sarah felt her cheeks flush, her heart racing. "You have such a gift for making people laugh. It's truly incredible."

Ethan chuckled, his eyes twinkling with appreciation. "Well, I believe laughter is the language of the heart. And speaking of which, I couldn't help but notice your infectious laughter from the stage. It's quite captivating."

Sarah couldn't help but giggle, feeling an instant connection with Ethan. "I've always believed that laughter is the key to a happy and fulfilled life. It's what brings people together and makes every moment memorable."

Ethan nodded, a hint of intrigue in his voice. "I couldn't agree more, Sarah. In fact, I've been looking for someone who shares my passion for laughter and joy. Someone who appreciates the comedic side of life."

Sarah's eyes widened, a mixture of excitement and curiosity filling her. "Are you saying what I think you're saying?"

Ethan grinned, leaning in closer. "I'm saying that I'd love to get to know you better, Sarah. Perhaps over a cup of coffee or a comedy show? What do you say?"

Sarah's heart soared with delight, her laughter bubbling up from within. "I'd love to, Ethan. Let's embark on a laughter-filled adventure together."

As Sarah and Ethan exchanged contact information and made plans for their first official date, a sense of joy and anticipation filled the air. Little did they know that their shared love for laughter would be the foundation of a romance that would unfold with countless humorous moments and heartfelt connections.

Chapter 3: The Meet-Cute

Sarah paced nervously outside the comedy club, her heart fluttering with a mix of excitement and anticipation. It was the night of her first date with Ethan, and she couldn't help but feel a delightful nervousness in her stomach.

As she waited, Ethan rounded the corner, wearing a mischievous grin that mirrored her own. He approached her with a playful twinkle in his eyes.

"Well, well, look who's here," Ethan said, his voice filled with charm. "Sarah, I must say, you clean up nicely."

Sarah chuckled, her eyes sparkling. "Why, thank you, Ethan. You're not looking too shabby yourself."

Ethan offered her his arm, a gesture that felt both natural and thrilling. "Shall we, my dear? I have a surprise in store for you."

Curiosity piqued, Sarah linked her arm with his, feeling an immediate connection. "I'm all ears, Ethan. Lead the way."

They strolled through the bustling city streets, engaging in witty banter and playful banter at every turn. The conversation flowed effortlessly, their minds dancing to the rhythm of laughter.

As they walked, Sarah couldn't help but be captivated by Ethan's quick wit and sharp sense of humor. Every word he spoke seemed to carry a touch of comedic brilliance, leaving her in awe of his talent.

Suddenly, they arrived at a dimly lit café tucked away on a quiet street corner. The aroma of freshly brewed coffee wafted through the air, welcoming them inside.

Ethan held the door open, a mischievous glint in his eyes. "Welcome to 'Jest-a-Latte,' Sarah. This place is known for its clever baristas and surprise comedy acts. I thought it would be the perfect setting for our first date."

Sarah's face lit up, her laughter bubbling up from within. "You certainly know how to pick a unique spot, Ethan. I can't wait to see what surprises await."

They found a cozy corner booth and settled in, their conversation continuing to flow effortlessly. The barista approached, their eyes twinkling with a playful energy.

"What can I get you two lovely comedians tonight?" the barista asked, a hint of mischief in their voice.

Ethan leaned back, feigning deep thought. "I'll have a 'Double Shot of Laughter' with a side of witty banter, please."

Sarah laughed, her eyes sparkling with amusement. "In that case, I'll have a 'Caffeinated Comedy' with extra chuckles, please."

The barista nodded, a wide smile spreading across their face. "Coming right up! Enjoy the show, lovebirds."

As they sipped their coffee, Sarah found herself falling deeper into the enchanting world of laughter that Ethan created. Their banter continued, blending seamlessly with the atmosphere of the café.

Hours flew by like minutes, and as they reluctantly left the café, a sense of undeniable chemistry hung in the air. Sarah couldn't help but feel that this was the beginning of something truly special—a love story written in the language of laughter.

AS SARAH AND ETHAN walked together, their laughter echoed through the city streets. Their connection felt effortless, and they couldn't help but revel in the joy they found in each other's company.

Just as they turned a corner, they stumbled upon a street performer who had gathered quite a crowd. The performer, a juggling clown with a mischievous grin, caught sight of Sarah and Ethan and motioned for them to join the spectacle.

"Step right up, ladies and gentlemen! We have two brave souls here who are about to embark on a comedy challenge!" the clown announced, his voice booming with enthusiasm.

Sarah looked at Ethan, a mixture of excitement and curiosity in her eyes. "What do you say, Ethan? Shall we embrace this unexpected twist and see where it takes us?"

Ethan flashed a grin, his eyes gleaming with adventure. "Why not, Sarah? Life is too short to resist the call of comedy. Let's give it a whirl!"

The crowd cheered as Sarah and Ethan stepped forward, ready to take on the challenge. The clown handed them each a set of juggling balls, a mischievous glint in his eyes.

"Now, the rules are simple," the clown explained. "You must pass the juggling balls back and forth between each other without dropping any. But there's a catch—you must also recite your favorite jokes while juggling!"

Sarah and Ethan exchanged a quick glance, their competitive spirits ignited. They began tossing the balls with determination, their comedic timing blending seamlessly with their juggling skills.

Sarah started, her voice filled with enthusiasm. "Why don't scientists trust atoms? Because they make up everything!"

The crowd erupted in laughter, spurring Ethan to continue. "I told my wife she should embrace her mistakes. She hugged me."

The laughter grew louder as Sarah caught the balls and replied, "Why don't skeletons fight each other? They don't have the guts!"

The performance continued, their jokes and juggling becoming more adventurous and daring with each passing moment. The onlookers were captivated, unable to tear their eyes away from the duo's comedic brilliance.

As the final punchline was delivered, Sarah and Ethan caught the balls simultaneously, their eyes meeting with a mix of exhilaration and triumph. The crowd erupted in applause and cheers, their appreciation for the spontaneous comedy act evident.

Breathing heavily, Sarah turned to Ethan, a wide grin on her face. "That was unexpected but absolutely amazing! Who knew juggling and jokes could go hand in hand?"

Ethan chuckled, wiping a bead of sweat from his brow. "I guess comedy has a way of surprising us, Sarah. It brings out the best in us, even in the most unexpected situations."

As the crowd dispersed, Sarah and Ethan found themselves standing alone on the street, their hearts still racing with excitement.

Sarah turned to Ethan, a newfound curiosity in her voice. "You know, Ethan, I think we make a pretty great team. Our connection and sense of humor seem to complement each other perfectly."

Ethan smiled, his eyes twinkling with delight. "I couldn't agree more, Sarah. Our comedic chemistry is undeniable. I can't wait to see what other adventures await us."

And so, with lingering laughter and a sense of wonder, Sarah and Ethan continued their journey, ready to embrace the unpredictable twists and turns of their love story.

SARAH AND ETHAN CONTINUED their lighthearted banter as they walked along the moonlit streets. Laughter filled the air, but beneath Sarah's radiant smile, a hint of hesitation lingered.

Ethan sensed a shift in Sarah's demeanor and gently touched her arm, his voice filled with concern. "Sarah, is something on your mind? You seem a little distant."

Sarah sighed, her eyes flickering with vulnerability. "Ethan, I've been having a wonderful time tonight, but I can't help but feel a tinge of fear creeping in. I've been hurt before, and the thought of putting myself out there again terrifies me."

Ethan's expression softened, understanding the weight of Sarah's words. He took a step closer, his voice gentle and reassuring. "Sarah,

I understand your fear. Love can be a risky endeavor, but if we let fear dictate our choices, we may miss out on something truly extraordinary. I promise to cherish and protect your heart, should you choose to give us a chance."

Sarah met Ethan's gaze, her eyes searching for sincerity. "It's not that I doubt your intentions, Ethan. It's just that past wounds can leave scars, and I'm afraid of reopening those old hurts."

Ethan reached out, his hand finding hers, offering comfort. "Sarah, scars are reminders of the battles we've fought and the strength we've gained. But they don't define our future. Together, we can create a new story—one filled with love, laughter, and healing."

Sarah's eyes shimmered with a mix of hope and apprehension. "You make it sound so easy, Ethan. But what if we stumble along the way? What if it doesn't work out?"

Ethan's thumb gently brushed against Sarah's hand, his voice filled with conviction. "Sarah, love is not without its challenges, but it's the willingness to face those challenges together that makes a relationship stronger. We'll stumble, we'll make mistakes, but as long as we communicate and support each other, we'll find our way. I believe in us."

Sarah's heart swayed with conflicting emotions. Ethan's words touched her deeply, resonating with a longing she had buried beneath her fears. She gazed into his eyes, silently contemplating her next step.

Finally, a smile tugged at the corners of her lips. "You know what, Ethan? You're right. Love is worth the risk. I don't want to let fear hold me back from experiencing something beautiful with you."

Ethan's face lit up, relief and joy washing over him. "Sarah, I'm thrilled to hear that. Let's embrace this journey together, one step at a time."

And so, hand in hand, Sarah and Ethan continued down the moonlit path, their laughter intertwining with newfound courage and vulnerability. With their hearts open to love's unpredictable dance, they embarked on a journey that promised both laughter and the possibility of healing.

Chapter 4: Humorous Antics

Sarah's life was an endless series of comedic misadventures and embarrassing moments. From tripping over her own feet in public to accidentally spilling coffee on herself, she seemed to attract laughter and amusement wherever she went.

One sunny morning, Sarah rushed out the door, already running late for work. As she hurried down the street, a gust of wind caught her skirt, causing it to billow up like a sail. Panicked, she attempted to hold it down, but her efforts only made the situation worse, leaving her hopping and twirling on the sidewalk like a comical dance routine.

Ethan, who happened to be passing by, couldn't help but burst into laughter at the sight. "Sarah, I've seen some impressive dance moves in my life, but that one takes the cake!"

Blushing furiously, Sarah managed to regain control of her skirt, smoothing it down with a sheepish grin. "Well, Ethan, I guess you can add 'Street Skirt Dancer' to my list of talents."

Ethan chuckled, his eyes twinkling with amusement. "You definitely know how to bring laughter into everyday situations, Sarah. It's one of the things I adore about you."

As they continued their walk, Sarah couldn't shake off the feeling that she was a magnet for comedic mishaps. Just as the thought crossed her mind, she stepped on a rogue banana peel, her feet flying out from under her. With a shriek, she landed on her backside, causing passersby to stop and stare.

Ethan rushed to her side, concern etched on his face. "Sarah, are you okay?"

Sarah groaned, rubbing her sore backside. "Well, I've always wondered how it feels to be in a slapstick comedy. Now I know."

Ethan helped her up, unable to contain his laughter. "You certainly know how to make an entrance, Sarah. I hope you're not hurt."

Sarah grinned, dusting off her clothes. "Just my pride, Ethan. I've learned to roll with the punches—or in this case, the banana peels."

Their laughter echoed through the street, turning Sarah's moment of embarrassment into a shared joke. It was in these lighthearted moments that their bond grew stronger, as they navigated life's whimsical twists together.

As they reached a café, Sarah's eyes widened with excitement. "Ethan, let's grab a cup of coffee. I promise not to spill it on myself this time."

Ethan chuckled, holding the door open for her. "I have faith in your coffee-carrying skills, Sarah. But even if you do spill, it'll just be another one of our memorable moments."

As they settled into a cozy corner of the café, Sarah couldn't help but feel grateful for the way Ethan embraced her quirks and turned them into laughter. In his company, even the most embarrassing moments became shared adventures, weaving a tapestry of love and laughter that would continue to unfold.

ETHAN HAD ALWAYS BEEN the calm and composed one, but his association with Sarah seemed to draw out his playful side. Wherever they went, laughter and hilarity followed in their wake.

One sunny afternoon, Sarah and Ethan decided to take a romantic stroll through a park. As they walked hand in hand, Sarah spotted a group of children gathered around a bubble machine, their eyes filled with wonder.

Unable to resist the temptation, Sarah tugged at Ethan's hand, her eyes sparkling mischievously. "Ethan, do you dare me to chase those bubbles?"

Ethan chuckled, his heart already racing with anticipation. "Sarah, you know I can't resist a dare. Go for it!"

With a burst of energy, Sarah dashed towards the bubbles, giggling like a child. Ethan followed close behind, his laughter blending with hers. They darted and weaved through the floating orbs, their arms outstretched as they tried to pop as many as possible.

Their infectious laughter caught the attention of other park-goers, who couldn't help but join in the joyous spectacle. Soon, a crowd had formed, cheering Sarah and Ethan on as they continued their bubble-popping spree.

As Sarah reached out to catch a particularly elusive bubble, she slipped on a patch of wet grass, her arms flailing in the air. Ethan lunged forward, managing to catch her just in time, but not without losing his balance in the process. The two of them tumbled to the ground in a heap of laughter.

Amidst their laughter-filled sprawl, Sarah looked up at Ethan, her eyes twinkling. "Well, Ethan, I guess we've taken bubble-popping to a whole new level."

Ethan grinned, his voice filled with amusement. "I've always believed in going the extra mile, Sarah. Even if it means ending up flat on the ground."

They burst into laughter once more, their shared mishap only deepening their connection. In each other's arms, they found solace in the unpredictability of life and the beauty of embracing every silly moment.

As they picked themselves up and brushed off the grass, Sarah couldn't help but feel a surge of gratitude for Ethan. His willingness to partake in these hilarious situations allowed her to fully be herself, quirks and all. In his presence, she discovered that laughter wasn't just a response to comedy—it was a bridge that connected their hearts.

With renewed energy, they continued their stroll through the park, hand in hand, their laughter echoing through the trees. In that moment, Sarah and Ethan knew that their love story was more than just romance—it was a delightful comedy of errors, written with laughter and sealed with a bond that grew stronger with each shared chuckle.

AS SARAH AND ETHAN continued their journey of love and laughter, their connection deepened, and a playful and flirtatious dynamic blossomed between them. Their conversations were filled with witty banter and teasing, each interaction leaving them longing for more.

One evening, Sarah and Ethan found themselves at a lively carnival. The air was filled with the scent of cotton candy and the sounds of laughter and music. Sarah's eyes sparkled with excitement as she spotted a game booth with a dartboard.

"Hey, Ethan," Sarah said, a mischievous glint in her eyes. "Wanna see if you can beat me at darts?"

Ethan raised an eyebrow, a playful challenge evident in his voice. "Oh, Sarah, I never back down from a challenge. You're on!"

They stepped up to the booth, each taking turns throwing darts, their competitive spirits in full swing. Sarah's first dart missed the target entirely, prompting Ethan to tease her.

"Looks like you've got a bit of a shaky aim there, Sarah. Need to work on your dart-throwing skills?"

Sarah shot him a playful glare. "Oh, just you wait, Ethan. I'm about to show you some real dart-throwing expertise!"

With renewed determination, Sarah's next dart hit the target dead center, earning her a cheer from the onlookers. Ethan's mock surprise was evident on his face.

"Well, well, Sarah. I didn't know you had hidden talents. Perhaps I should be worried."

Sarah smirked, reveling in her small victory. "Oh, you should be worried, Ethan. You're about to witness a dart-throwing master in action!"

Their playful banter continued as they took turns throwing darts, each trying to outdo the other. The crowd around them grew, cheering and laughing at their antics. It didn't matter who won; what mattered was the joy they found in each other's company and the way their playful dynamic brought them closer.

As the night wore on, Sarah and Ethan explored the carnival hand in hand, trying their luck at various games and indulging in sweet treats. Their laughter echoed through the colorful attractions, creating a bubble of happiness around them.

At a photo booth, they squeezed into a tiny space, their faces pressed close together. As the countdown began, Sarah couldn't resist a mischievous whisper.

"Let's make this a memorable photo, Ethan. Ready?"

Ethan nodded, a grin dancing on his lips. "Absolutely, Sarah. Show me what you've got."

As the camera clicked, Sarah planted a surprise kiss on Ethan's cheek, capturing a moment of playful affection. Their laughter erupted once more, filling the booth and floating out into the carnival.

In that moment, Sarah and Ethan knew that their connection was more than just lighthearted fun—it was a dance of flirtation and shared joy. Their playful dynamic brought a sparkle to their eyes and an electricity to their touch, leaving no doubt that love and laughter were intertwined in their hearts.

Chapter 5: The Obstacle

Sarah and Ethan had danced through a whirlwind of love and laughter, their connection growing stronger with each passing day. But like any great love story, they were about to face their first major hurdle—a misunderstanding that threatened to create a rift between them.

One sunny afternoon, Sarah received an invitation to an art exhibition. Excitement filled her as she imagined sharing the experience with Ethan. She dialed his number, her finger hovering over the call button.

"Hey, Ethan! I just got an invitation to an art exhibition. I thought it would be a wonderful opportunity for us to spend some time together and appreciate beautiful art. What do you think?"

There was a brief pause on the other end of the line, followed by a hesitant response. "Oh, Sarah, that sounds great, but I'm not really into art. I'm not sure if it's my thing."

Sarah's heart sank, her mind immediately jumping to conclusions. "Oh, I see. I thought you would enjoy it. Maybe we can do something else then."

Ethan, sensing her disappointment, tried to explain himself. "No, Sarah, that's not what I meant. It's just that art isn't my forte, but if it's important to you, I'll go with you. I want to share these experiences with you."

But Sarah, already hurt by her own assumptions, didn't give him a chance to clarify. "No, Ethan, it's fine. I don't want you to feel obligated to do something you're not interested in. I'll find someone else to go with."

With that, she hung up the phone, leaving Ethan bewildered and pained by the sudden rift between them.

Days turned into weeks, and silence settled between Sarah and Ethan. Their usual playful banter and laughter were replaced by an unspoken tension that weighed heavy on their hearts. Miscommunication had driven a wedge between them, leaving them both yearning for resolution.

AS SARAH AND ETHAN worked through their miscommunication and sought to reconnect, their well-meaning friends saw an opportunity to help. However, their attempts at reconciliation were far from smooth, leading to a series of comedic mishaps.

One sunny afternoon, Sarah's best friend, Lily, decided to take matters into her own hands. Armed with her enthusiasm and a plan, she approached Ethan at a local café.

"Ethan, my dear friend, I believe it's time to mend the bridge between you and Sarah," Lily declared, wearing a mischievous grin.

Ethan looked up from his cup of coffee, his curiosity piqued. "Lily, I appreciate your intentions, but I think Sarah and I are working things out on our own."

Lily waved off his concerns. "Nonsense! I have a foolproof plan. We're going to set up a surprise encounter. Trust me, it's going to be amazing!"

Ethan's skepticism grew, but he couldn't help but be intrigued by Lily's confidence. "Alright, Lily. I'm willing to hear you out. What's your plan?"

Lily leaned in, her voice barely above a whisper. "We'll arrange for both of you to attend a charity event. You'll be dressed to the nines, and at the perfect moment, I'll orchestrate a grand entrance for Sarah. The sight of her in that stunning gown will melt your heart, and all misunderstandings will disappear."

Ethan furrowed his brow, trying to picture the scenario. "Lily, I appreciate the effort, but won't it be too contrived? I think Sarah and I need genuine moments to reconnect, not orchestrated ones."

Lily waved away his concerns once again, her eyes sparkling with determination. "Trust me, Ethan. This plan has a 99% success rate in romantic comedies. What could go wrong?"

Reluctantly, Ethan agreed to Lily's plan, hoping that perhaps her enthusiasm would work some magic. Little did he know that chaos was about to ensue.

On the night of the charity event, Sarah nervously stepped into the elegant ballroom, unaware of Lily's well-intentioned scheme. She wore a stunning gown, feeling a mix of excitement and trepidation about seeing Ethan again.

Meanwhile, Lily, who had taken on the role of the matchmaker extraordinaire, scurried around the ballroom, orchestrating the perfect moment for Sarah's grand entrance. She signaled the DJ, who queued the romantic music as the crowd hushed in anticipation.

But just as Sarah was about to make her entrance, her heel got caught in the hem of her gown, causing her to stumble forward. The room erupted in gasps and laughter as Sarah desperately clung to a nearby table, trying to regain her balance.

Ethan, who happened to be nearby, rushed to Sarah's aid, his concern evident on his face. "Sarah, are you alright? Let me help."

Sarah, her cheeks flushing with embarrassment, managed a sheepish smile. "I'm fine, Ethan. Just a little mishap with my gown. Thank you for saving me from a complete disaster."

As they shared a laugh and tried to untangle Sarah's dress, Lily watched from a distance, her eyes wide with disbelief. Her plan had backfired spectacularly, but in that moment, she realized something important—genuine moments were far more powerful than any orchestrated encounter.

With a sigh of relief, Lily decided to let go of her matchmaking endeavors and let Sarah and Ethan navigate their relationship on their own terms. Sometimes, love needed room to breathe and grow naturally, without the interference of well-meaning but misguided friends.

AS SARAH AND ETHAN navigated the aftermath of their misunderstanding, Sarah found herself reflecting on her true feelings for him. In the midst of the chaos and miscommunication, she had discovered just how much Ethan meant to her. Determined to win him back, she embarked on a journey of self-discovery and heartfelt determination.

One evening, Sarah sat alone in her favorite coffee shop, a steaming cup of chai in her hands. She stared out of the window, lost in her thoughts, replaying the moments she had shared with Ethan.

"I can't deny it any longer," Sarah whispered to herself. "I've fallen for him, head over heels. He's become such an important part of my life, and I miss his laughter, his presence, his kindness."

With newfound clarity, Sarah realized that she had taken Ethan for granted, assuming that their connection would always be there. But now, she understood the fragility of love and the importance of fighting for what truly mattered.

Determined to win Ethan back, Sarah picked up her phone and dialed his number. She took a deep breath, her heart pounding in her chest, as she waited for him to answer.

"Ethan, it's me, Sarah," she began, her voice filled with a mix of nervousness and determination. "I want to apologize once again for my assumptions and jumping to conclusions. But more importantly, I want to tell you something. I've realized just how much you mean to me."

On the other end of the line, Ethan listened attentively, his own heart racing with anticipation. "Go on, Sarah. I'm listening."

Tears welled up in Sarah's eyes, her voice trembling with emotion. "Ethan, you've brought so much joy and laughter into my life. I miss us, I miss our connection, and I miss being by your side. I want to fight for us, for our love and laughter."

There was a brief pause, followed by a deep sigh from Ethan. "Sarah, I've missed you too. I've been wrestling with my own feelings, unsure of how to bridge the gap between us. But hearing your words, I realize that I still love you, despite the misunderstandings."

Sarah's heart soared with hope, her determination solidifying. "Ethan, let's not let miscommunication define us. Let's come together and work through our challenges. I'm ready to fight for us, to fight for the love and laughter we share."

Ethan's voice softened with warmth. "Sarah, I want nothing more than to be by your side. Let's rebuild our connection, one honest conversation at a time."

In that moment, Sarah and Ethan knew that their love story wasn't over. It was merely taking a detour, a journey of growth and understanding. With newfound clarity and a deepened commitment to each other, they set out on a path to rediscover the love and laughter that had brought them together.

Chapter 6: The Romantic Rival

As Sarah and Ethan set out to restore their love and laughter, a new challenge emerges in the form of a charismatic rival vying for Ethan's affections. It's Alex, a charming and witty character who effortlessly attracts the attention of those around her.

One sunny afternoon, Sarah and Ethan found themselves attending a local art exhibition, hoping to immerse themselves in creativity and inspiration. Little did they know that this outing would introduce them to a charismatic force that would test the strength of their connection.

As they strolled through the gallery, admiring the vibrant paintings and sculptures, Sarah noticed a crowd gathering around a particular artwork. Curiosity piqued, she tugged on Ethan's arm, urging him to join the throng.

"There must be something amazing to attract such a crowd," Sarah said, her eyes sparkling with anticipation.

Ethan nodded, his gaze fixed on the painting that had captivated the attention of everyone present. "It's quite captivating, indeed."

Just as they approached the artwork, a voice spoke up from behind them. "Ah, I see you're admiring the masterpiece as well. Quite a remarkable piece, isn't it?"

Sarah and Ethan turned, their eyes meeting the gaze of a charming stranger. He had a mischievous smile and a twinkle in his eyes that seemed to invite intrigue.

"Yes, it's truly stunning," Sarah replied, her voice laced with curiosity.

The stranger extended her hand, introducing herself as Alex. "I couldn't help but overhear your conversation. I must say, art is a wonderful way to connect with one's emotions. I'm quite the enthusiast myself."

Ethan, always polite, shook Alex's hand, a polite smile on his face. "Nice to meet you, Alex. I'm Ethan, and this is Sarah."

Sarah observed the easy banter between Ethan and Alex, a twinge of unease creeping into her heart. She had always trusted Ethan, but the undeniable charm of this newcomer made her question her own confidence.

As they continued their conversation, Sarah found herself growing increasingly aware of the connection between Alex and Ethan. Their shared interests and quick wit seemed to form an undeniable bond, leaving Sarah feeling like an outsider.

In the days that followed, Alex made several appearances in Sarah and Ethan's lives, effortlessly integrating herself into their circle of friends. She was always present, engaging everyone with his charm and infectious laughter.

Sarah couldn't help but feel a pang of jealousy, her mind filled with doubt and insecurities. She longed for the easy laughter and connection she and Ethan had shared, fearing that Alex's presence would disrupt their delicate balance.

One evening, as they sat in a cozy café, Sarah finally mustered the courage to address her concerns. She looked into Ethan's eyes, her voice tinged with vulnerability. "Ethan, I can't help but feel threatened by Alex. It seems like she has a special connection with you, and it's making me question our own bond."

Ethan reached across the table, gently taking Sarah's hand in his. "Sarah, I understand your concerns, but I want to assure you that my feelings for you haven't wavered. Alex may be charming, but our connection is something unique and irreplaceable. Trust me, I'm committed to us."

Sarah felt a wave of relief wash over her, a renewed sense of trust blossoming within her heart. She squeezed Ethan's hand, a smile tugging at her lips. "Thank you, Ethan. I needed to hear that. Let's not allow a charming rival to overshadow what we have."

With their love and laughter fortified, Sarah and Ethan faced the challenge of Alex's presence together, united in their determination to protect the unique magic they shared.

AS SARAH GRAPPLED WITH her insecurities about the charming rival, Alex, she decided to take a lighthearted approach to the situation. Determined to outwit and outshine him, she embarked on a series of humorous attempts to reclaim her place in Ethan's heart.

One sunny afternoon, Sarah and Ethan found themselves at a local park, enjoying a picnic under the shade of a sprawling oak tree. As they laughed and shared stories, Sarah noticed Alex approaching in the distance, a mischievous grin on her face.

Feeling a surge of determination, Sarah turned to Ethan with a sly smile. "Watch and learn, Ethan. It's time to bring out my secret weapon."

Ethan raised an eyebrow, his curiosity piqued. "What are you up to, Sarah?"

Sarah rummaged through her bag and pulled out a tiny handheld fan. With a twinkle in her eye, she turned it on, causing a gentle breeze to flutter through her hair. She then proceeded to strike a pose, pretending to be caught in a dramatic movie scene.

"Ah, the wind in my hair, the sun on my face," Sarah exclaimed dramatically. "I shall call this move 'The Breezy Diversion.'"

Ethan burst into laughter, unable to contain his amusement. "Sarah, you're absolutely ridiculous!"

Sarah winked at him playfully. "Exactly! And that's precisely the point. I'm going to show Alex that I can be just as charming and entertaining."

As Alex drew nearer, Sarah continued her theatrics, mimicking her charm with exaggerated gestures and witty remarks. She engaged everyone around her in conversation, leaving them in fits of laughter.

Alex, taken aback by Sarah's humorous antics, couldn't help but be impressed. She approached the picnic blanket, a mixture of amusement and curiosity on her face. "Well, well, Sarah. I must say, you certainly know how to command attention."

Sarah grinned, her eyes sparkling with mischief. "Why, thank you, Alex. I thought I'd give you a taste of my charm. After all, it's not easy being the life of the party."

Ethan chuckled, joining in on the playful banter. "Looks like we have a competition on our hands, Alex. Sarah's comedy skills are unmatched."

Alex laughed, a twinkle of admiration in his eyes. "Indeed, Ethan. Sarah's humor is a force to be reckoned with. But let's not forget the power of genuine connections and shared laughter."

Throughout their encounters, Sarah continued her humorous attempts to outshine Alex, whether it was engaging in impromptu dance-offs or reciting cheesy pick-up lines. Each time, she managed to bring a sense of lightness and laughter to their interactions.

As the days passed, Sarah's humorous endeavors not only entertained those around her but also reminded Ethan of the unique bond they shared. It was a testament to the strength of their connection and the power of laughter in their relationship.

AS SARAH PLAYFULLY attempted to outwit and outshine the charismatic rival, Alex, Ethan found himself caught in a web of growing confusion and internal conflict. His heart was torn between the familiarity and depth of his connection with Sarah and the undeniable allure of Alex's charm.

Late one evening, as Ethan sat alone in his apartment, he stared at the flickering candle on his coffee table, lost in thought. The events of the past few days had left him questioning his own emotions and the path he should choose.

He picked up his phone and dialed Sarah's number, hoping to find some clarity in their conversation. After a few rings, she answered, her voice filled with warmth. "Hey, Ethan, what's on your mind?"

Ethan hesitated for a moment, unsure of how to express the turmoil within him. He took a deep breath and began, "Sarah, I need to talk. I feel torn between my feelings for you and this unexpected connection I have with Alex. It's confusing, and I don't want to hurt either of you."

Sarah, her voice filled with understanding, replied, "Ethan, it's normal to feel conflicted when faced with unexpected emotions. What matters is how we navigate through it together. Let's talk it out, honestly and openly."

Ethan sighed, grateful for Sarah's unwavering support. "I care about both of you, Sarah. Our history, the laughter we've shared—it's undeniable. But Alex, she's like a breath of fresh air, stirring something new within me. It's a struggle to reconcile these conflicting emotions."

Sarah's voice remained steady, her love shining through her words. "Ethan, love isn't always straightforward. It's okay to feel confused. What's important is that we communicate and listen to our hearts. Remember, we're in this together."

Ethan nodded, even though Sarah couldn't see him. "You're right, Sarah. I don't want to lose what we have. Our connection is irreplaceable. But I also need to explore this new path and understand my feelings for Alex. It's a delicate balance."

Sarah's voice filled with compassion. "Take the time you need, Ethan. Know that my love for you is unwavering, no matter what path you choose. We'll figure it out together, one step at a time."

As the conversation ended, Ethan felt a mixture of relief and uncertainty. He knew that he needed to navigate this internal conflict with honesty and sensitivity. It was a journey of self-discovery, one that would test his own understanding of love and his commitment to both Sarah and himself.

In the days that followed, Ethan found himself reflecting on his encounters with both Sarah and Alex, searching for clarity amidst the emotional whirlwind. He questioned what truly mattered to him, what kind of love he sought—whether it was the deep-rooted comfort he had with Sarah or the exhilarating spontaneity he experienced with Alex.

With each passing day, Ethan's confusion grew, but he remained determined to navigate his feelings with honesty and integrity. The battle for his heart raged on, leaving him introspective, uncertain, and on the precipice of a life-altering decision.

Chapter 7: Heartfelt Moments

In the midst of confusion and uncertainty, Sarah and Ethan found solace in each other's presence. They embarked on a journey of introspection, opening their hearts and engaging in vulnerable conversations that deepened their emotional connection.

One evening, as the sun set and cast a warm, golden glow over the city, Sarah and Ethan found themselves on a quiet rooftop overlooking the bustling streets below. The gentle breeze carried their voices as they sat side by side, their hands intertwined.

Ethan turned to Sarah, his eyes filled with vulnerability. "Sarah, I've been soul-searching for days, trying to understand my feelings. But the more I reflect, the more I realize that you're the one who knows me best. You've seen me at my happiest and my lowest. You've been with me through it all."

Sarah squeezed Ethan's hand, offering him a reassuring smile. "Ethan, our connection goes beyond the surface. We've shared laughter and tears, dreams and fears. It's a bond that's been tested and strengthened over time. I believe in the power of our love."

Ethan's voice trembled with emotion as he continued, "And what about Alex? Sarah, I can't ignore the way he makes me feel. He challenges me, pushes me out of my comfort zone. But with you, it's like coming home."

Sarah's eyes shimmered with unshed tears as she spoke, her voice filled with unwavering love. "Ethan, love doesn't always follow a predictable path. It's messy, complicated, and sometimes it takes us by surprise. But what truly matters is the depth of our connection, the honesty and vulnerability we share."

Ethan leaned closer, his forehead resting against Sarah's. "You're right, Sarah. Our love has stood the test of time, and through these conversations, I realize how deeply I cherish it. It's not about choosing between two people; it's about choosing the kind of love that brings us the most fulfillment."

Sarah's voice was soft but resolute. "Ethan, we can navigate this together. We can communicate, support each other, and discover the path that aligns our hearts. Love is not about perfection—it's about the willingness to grow, adapt, and embrace the unknown."

As the night sky enveloped them, Sarah and Ethan found comfort in their shared vulnerability. They allowed themselves to be open, to express their deepest fears and desires, knowing that their love had the strength to withstand any challenge.

In the days that followed, Sarah and Ethan continued their heartfelt conversations, diving into the depths of their souls and exploring their dreams and aspirations. They laughed, they cried, and they discovered new layers of understanding within themselves and each other.

Their emotional connection grew stronger with each passing day, reminding them that the power of love and laughter lies not in avoiding challenges, but in facing them together with unwavering support and understanding.

AS SARAH AND ETHAN delved deeper into their heartfelt conversations, they stumbled upon a poignant moment—a realization that their values and dreams aligned more than they had ever anticipated.

One sunny afternoon, they decided to take a stroll through a nearby park, hand in hand. The vibrant colors of blooming flowers surrounded them, creating a picturesque backdrop for their conversation.

Sarah turned to Ethan, her eyes sparkling with excitement. "Ethan, you know, as we've been talking, I've realized that our dreams and values are remarkably similar. It's like we've been dancing around the same aspirations without even knowing it."

Ethan's curiosity piqued, and he smiled at Sarah. "Tell me more, Sarah. What do you mean?"

Sarah's voice grew animated as she began to paint a vivid picture of their shared dreams. "Ethan, remember that conversation we had about traveling the world? It turns out we both have a deep desire to explore new cultures, immerse ourselves in different experiences, and create unforgettable memories together."

Ethan's eyes widened with surprise and admiration. "You're right, Sarah. I've always wanted to travel, to witness the beauty of different landscapes and connect with people from diverse backgrounds. The thought of embarking on adventures with you fills me with joy."

Sarah's smile widened, and she continued, "And then there's the way we value laughter and finding joy in the simplest of moments. We both believe in the power of humor to heal, to bring people together, and to turn even the darkest days into something lighter and brighter."

Ethan nodded, his heart swelling with warmth. "Absolutely, Sarah. Laughter has been our lifeline, our secret language. It's something we've shared from the very beginning, and it's a treasure I never want to lose."

Sarah's voice grew softer as she shared her final discovery. "Ethan, when we talked about making a positive impact on the world, it felt like our souls were singing in harmony. We both have a deep desire to leave this world a better place, to touch lives and make a difference, no matter how big or small."

Ethan's gaze locked with Sarah's, filled with admiration and a newfound sense of connection. "Sarah, I've always admired your compassion and your dedication to helping others. It's a quality that drew me to you from the start. And now, to know that we share this vision—it's truly extraordinary."

As they continued their walk through the park, Sarah and Ethan felt a profound sense of unity. Their shared dreams and values had woven an unbreakable bond between them, deepening their love and igniting a newfound sense of purpose.

In the days that followed, Sarah and Ethan embarked on explorations of their shared dreams, discussing the places they wished to visit, the laughter they yearned to create, and the ways they could make a positive impact on the world together.

Their poignant moment of discovery had illuminated the path ahead, showing them that their love and laughter were not just sources of joy but also catalysts for growth and fulfillment.

SARAH AND ETHAN FOUND themselves in a moment of quiet reflection, their hearts brimming with a profound realization. Their connection, which had initially been built on laughter, had transcended into something deeper—an unbreakable bond that touched their souls.

One evening, they decided to take a break from their busy lives and enjoy a cozy night in. Sarah had prepared a delicious homemade dinner, and as they sat at the candlelit table, their gazes met, filled with a mix of playfulness and tenderness.

Ethan took a deep breath, breaking the comfortable silence that enveloped them. "Sarah, I can't help but marvel at how our connection has evolved. Laughter brought us together, but it's become so much more than that. It's like we have this invisible thread that intertwines our hearts, binding us in a way that defies explanation."

Sarah's eyes sparkled with understanding, and she reached across the table to clasp Ethan's hand. "Ethan, I couldn't agree more. Our laughter was the spark, the magnetic force that drew us closer. But as we've shared our hopes, dreams, fears, and vulnerabilities, it's become evident that our connection runs deep, reaching the very core of who we are."

Ethan's voice was filled with wonder as he spoke, "It's as if our souls recognize each other, Sarah. Beyond the laughter, we've discovered a sense of comfort, trust, and understanding that is rare and precious. It's like we've known each other for a lifetime, even though our paths crossed only recently."

Sarah nodded, her expression softening with affection. "Yes, Ethan. And it's not just the good times that have strengthened our bond. It's the way we've stood by each other through the challenges, offering support and unwavering love. We've seen each other's vulnerabilities and imperfections, yet we choose to embrace them wholeheartedly."

Ethan's grip tightened around Sarah's hand, his voice filled with sincerity. "Sarah, I believe that love is not just about the laughter—it's about finding someone who sees you, who accepts you for who you truly are. It's about feeling safe to be your authentic self and knowing that you're cherished and loved in return."

Sarah's heart swelled with warmth, her voice gentle and unwavering. "Ethan, our connection is rooted in authenticity and vulnerability. It's about creating a space where we can be our true selves, where we can share our dreams, fears, and insecurities without judgment. It's a love that celebrates our individuality and encourages personal growth."

As they continued to share heartfelt conversations, Sarah and Ethan marveled at the depth of their connection, recognizing that their love and laughter were intertwined, forming a tapestry of unwavering support and unconditional acceptance.

In the days that followed, they cherished the moments of laughter and joy, savoring the lightness they brought to each other's lives. But they also reveled in the quiet moments—the shared glances, the gentle touches, and the profound understanding that only true soulmates can experience.

Their realization that their connection transcended laughter and delved into something deeper filled their hearts with gratitude and a renewed commitment to nurture their love.

Chapter 8: Relationship Challenges

Sarah Thompson and Ethan Reynolds had always been a picture-perfect couple, their love story filled with laughter, shared dreams, and stolen moments. But as they delved deeper into their relationship, they began to face the realities and challenges that come with love.

One sunny Saturday afternoon, Sarah and Ethan decided to take a stroll through the local park, hand in hand. As they walked along the winding path, their footsteps falling in sync, Sarah couldn't help but feel a knot of uncertainty forming in her stomach. She had been holding onto a secret, one that she knew could potentially shake the foundation of their relationship.

With a sigh, she turned to Ethan, her eyes searching for courage. "Ethan, we need to talk," she said, her voice filled with trepidation.

Ethan's brow furrowed, concern etching deep lines on his face. "What's troubling you, Sarah? You seem distant lately."

Sarah took a deep breath, her heart pounding in her chest. "I... I've been offered a job opportunity in a different city," she admitted, her voice barely above a whisper. "It's a once-in-a-lifetime chance, but it would mean leaving everything behind, including you."

Ethan's grip on Sarah's hand tightened, his eyes filled with a mix of surprise and sadness. "Leaving? But what about us, Sarah? I can't imagine my life without you."

Tears welled up in Sarah's eyes as she met Ethan's gaze. "I feel the same way, Ethan. But this opportunity... it could change our lives in so many ways. I don't want to hold you back from your own dreams."

Ethan's voice softened as he pulled Sarah into a tight embrace. "Sarah, I love you more than anything. If this job is something that will make you happy, then I don't want to stand in your way. We'll find a way to make it work, no matter the distance."

Sarah clung to Ethan, her heart torn between her dreams and the love they shared. "But what if the distance becomes too much for us? What if it changes us?"

Ethan pulled back slightly, his gaze unwavering. "We'll face the challenges together, Sarah. We'll communicate, trust each other, and make an effort to bridge the gap. Love can conquer distance if we let it."

Sarah nodded, her tears mingling with a bittersweet smile. "You're right, Ethan. Our love is strong, and I believe in us. We'll navigate this new chapter in our lives and come out even stronger."

With renewed determination, they continued their walk through the park, their hands still intertwined. Sarah and Ethan knew that the road ahead wouldn't be easy, but they also understood that love was a force that could withstand any test.

Little did they know that their journey was about to become even more challenging, as life had a way of throwing unexpected curveballs their way. But armed with unwavering love and a shared commitment, Sarah and Ethan were ready to face whatever challenges lay ahead, hand in hand.

SARAH AND ETHAN WERE a couple who shared a love that was deep and sincere. But amidst their love for each other, they also discovered that they had their fair share of differences. These differences often led to hilarious disagreements and the need for compromises as they navigated the path of their relationship.

One evening, Sarah and Ethan found themselves in the midst of a lighthearted argument over something seemingly trivial—decorating their new apartment. Sarah had a flair for bright colors and bold patterns, while Ethan preferred a more minimalist and neutral aesthetic.

As they stood in the middle of the living room, surrounded by paint swatches and fabric samples, their voices rose in playful banter.

"I think this wall should be painted a vibrant shade of turquoise," Sarah declared, holding up a paint sample that seemed to glow with intensity.

Ethan shook his head, a smirk playing on his lips. "Turquoise? Are you trying to turn our living room into an underwater paradise?"

Sarah crossed her arms, her eyes gleaming mischievously. "Oh, come on, Ethan! It'll add a pop of color and make the room feel alive. We can balance it out with some neutral furniture."

Ethan raised an eyebrow, a mock serious expression on his face. "Neutral furniture? So, we're going for the 'underwater paradise meets Scandinavian minimalism' look?"

They burst into laughter, the tension of their disagreement melting away. It was in these moments of playful banter that they truly appreciated the joy they found in each other's company.

After a moment, Sarah's laughter subsided, and she took Ethan's hand in hers. "Okay, maybe turquoise isn't the best idea. But can we compromise? How about a light blue shade that evokes a sense of calm without overwhelming the room?"

Ethan nodded, a smile tugging at the corners of his lips. "That sounds reasonable. And in return, can we incorporate a few bold accents, like a vibrant rug or some colorful throw pillows?"

Sarah's eyes lit up, her excitement evident. "Deal! We'll create a space that reflects both of our personalities and makes us feel at home."

And so, armed with compromise and a shared sense of humor, Sarah and Ethan embarked on their quest to make their new apartment a reflection of their love and individuality. They spent hours browsing through furniture stores, debating color schemes, and laughing at their own quirks.

In the end, their apartment became a beautiful blend of Sarah's vibrant energy and Ethan's minimalist sensibilities. It was a space that represented their shared journey, filled with laughter, compromise, and the understanding that their differences were what made their love story truly unique.

As they sat on their newly decorated couch, Sarah leaned her head on Ethan's shoulder, a contented smile on her face. "You know, Ethan, our disagreements may be hilarious, but it's the compromises we make that remind me how perfectly imperfect we are together."

"Absolutely, Sarah. Our love is a beautiful dance of compromise, laughter, and everything in between. And I wouldn't have it any other way."

SARAH THOMPSON AND Ethan Reynolds had always believed their love was unbreakable, but as they journeyed through their relationship, they couldn't escape the occasional moments of doubt and insecurity that crept into their hearts.

One evening, as they sat at their favorite coffee shop, sipping their respective drinks, a heavy silence settled between them. Sarah fidgeted with her coffee cup, her gaze fixed on the table, her thoughts swirling with uncertainty.

Ethan reached out and gently took her hand, his eyes filled with concern. "Sarah, what's troubling you? You seem distant today."

Sarah sighed, her voice barely above a whisper. "I can't help but wonder if I'm enough for you, Ethan. I see the way other women look at you, and sometimes I feel like I pale in comparison. What if one day, you realize you deserve someone better?"

Ethan's brow furrowed, his grip on Sarah's hand tightening. "Sarah, you are more than enough for me. Those women you're talking about, they don't hold a candle to the love and connection we share. I chose you for a reason, and it's because I see your beauty, inside and out."

Tears welled up in Sarah's eyes as she met Ethan's unwavering gaze. "But what if I can't live up to your expectations? What if I let you down?"

Ethan's voice softened as he brushed his thumb against the back of Sarah's hand. "Sarah, you don't have to be perfect. We all have our flaws and insecurities. What matters is that we support each other, lift each other up, and grow together. I'm here because I believe in us, in our love. And I'm not going anywhere."

Sarah's tears spilled over, a mixture of relief and vulnerability washing over her. "Thank you, Ethan. I needed to hear that. Sometimes, these doubts just get the better of me."

Ethan leaned closer, his voice filled with sincerity. "I understand, Sarah. We all have our moments of doubt. But remember, love is not about being flawless; it's about accepting each other's imperfections and choosing to love fiercely despite them."

As Sarah wiped away her tears, a small smile tugged at the corners of her lips. "You have a way of making everything clearer, Ethan. I'm grateful to have you by my side."

Ethan's smile matched hers as he gently brushed a strand of hair behind Sarah's ear. "And I'm grateful to have you in my life, Sarah. Our moments of doubt only serve to remind us of the strength of our commitment. We'll face them together, and our love will emerge even stronger."

With their doubts and insecurities laid bare, Sarah and Ethan found solace in the unconditional love they shared. It was in these vulnerable moments that their commitment to one another was tested, and with each passing challenge, their bond grew deeper.

As they continued their evening at the coffee shop, the air between them felt lighter, infused with renewed trust and a newfound appreciation for their love. Sarah and Ethan knew that doubts may arise again in the future, but armed with their unwavering commitment and open communication, they were ready to face any test that came their way.

Chapter 9: Happily Ever After

Chapter X: Happily Ever After

A. Resolution of conflicts and a stronger bond between Sarah and Ethan.

After navigating through various challenges in their relationship, Sarah Thompson and Ethan Reynolds found themselves at a point where the conflicts they faced had been resolved, leaving them with a stronger and more resilient bond than ever before.

One sunny afternoon, Sarah and Ethan sat on a blanket in the park, enjoying a picnic together. The gentle breeze rustled through the leaves, creating a soothing soundtrack to their conversation.

Sarah's eyes sparkled as she looked at Ethan, her voice filled with affection. "Remember when we used to argue about small things like who should control the TV remote? It's amazing how far we've come since then."

Ethan chuckled, his gaze fixed on Sarah. "Oh, I remember those days. We've certainly grown, haven't we? Resolving conflicts and finding common ground has become second nature to us."

Sarah nodded, a soft smile playing on her lips. "It's because we've learned to communicate better and truly listen to each other. We've realized that our love is worth fighting for, even when it's tough."

Ethan reached out and took Sarah's hand, his touch warm and reassuring. "Absolutely, Sarah. Our love is a journey, and along the way, we've discovered the importance of compromise, understanding, and forgiveness. It's these lessons that have brought us closer."

Sarah's gaze turned thoughtful as she traced circles on Ethan's palm. "And through it all, we've discovered parts of ourselves that we never knew existed. Our conflicts have shown us our strengths and weaknesses, allowing us to grow both individually and as a couple."

Ethan's eyes softened, his voice filled with tenderness. "You're right, Sarah. Every challenge we faced has made us stronger. We've learned to lean on each other, to support and uplift one another. Our bond has deepened, and our love has become even more profound."

As they sat there, basking in the warmth of the sun and the depth of their connection, Sarah and Ethan knew that their journey was not over. They understood that conflicts might arise again, but they were confident that they had the tools and the love necessary to overcome any obstacle.

In that moment, Sarah leaned her head on Ethan's shoulder, a contented sigh escaping her lips. "I'm grateful for the conflicts we've faced, Ethan. They've brought us to where we are today, and I wouldn't change a thing."

Ethan wrapped his arm around Sarah, his voice filled with unwavering devotion. "Me neither, Sarah. Our journey has been filled with ups and downs, but it's those moments of resolution and growth that have shaped our love into something truly extraordinary."

With their conflicts resolved and their bond strengthened, Sarah and Ethan continued their picnic in the park, savoring the simple joy of being together. They knew that their happily ever after was not a destination but a continuous adventure, one that they were eager to embark on hand in hand.

And as they laughed, shared stories, and dreamed of the future, Sarah and Ethan were ready to face whatever challenges lay ahead, knowing that their love was resilient, unbreakable, and destined to unravel the deepest strings of their hearts.

SARAH AND ETHAN HAD come a long way in their journey of love. They had faced numerous challenges and resolved conflicts, but there was one final obstacle that awaited them—an obstacle that would test their patience, love, and sense of humor.

It was a beautiful summer day, and Sarah and Ethan decided to embark on a much-anticipated road trip. As they packed their bags and loaded up the car, excitement filled the air. Little did they know that their adventure would take an unexpected turn.

They had been driving for a few hours when they found themselves on a desolate road in the middle of nowhere. The engine sputtered, and the car came to a halt with a loud clunk.

Ethan glanced at Sarah, his eyebrows raised in surprise. "Well, this is unexpected. Looks like we've encountered our final obstacle, Sarah."

Sarah sighed, a mix of frustration and amusement evident in her voice. "Of all the times for the car to break down, it had to be now. But hey, at least we have each other, right?"

Ethan smiled, his eyes twinkling mischievously. "Absolutely. And we have the power of our combined problem-solving skills. Let's figure this out, partner."

They stepped out of the car and peered under the hood, both of them clueless about the intricacies of automobile mechanics. Sarah couldn't help but giggle at the absurdity of the situation.

"Alright, Ethan, let's assess the situation. I see a lot of engine parts that I can't name, and I have no idea what to do," Sarah said, a playful grin on her face.

Ethan scratched his head, pretending to examine the engine intently. "Hmm, it seems we have a classic case of a broken doohickey here. We'll need some duct tape, a paperclip, and maybe a touch of magic to fix it."

Sarah burst into laughter, her eyes crinkling with joy. "Magic, huh? Well, I do possess a bit of wizardry. Let's give it a try!"

Together, they scoured the car, finding an assortment of random objects. Armed with duct tape, a paperclip, and their shared determination, they attempted to fix the "broken doohickey."

As they worked side by side, laughter and banter filled the air, temporarily overshadowing the frustration of the situation. Their comedic attempts at car repairs seemed to bring them closer, strengthening their bond even further.

After what felt like an eternity of tinkering and laughter, Sarah and Ethan stepped back, their masterpiece of makeshift repairs complete.

Ethan wiped his hands on a rag, a wide grin on his face. "Well, Sarah, I think we've done it. The car might not be in its prime, but it should get us to the nearest town."

Sarah beamed at him, a mix of pride and relief in her eyes. "Who knew we had a hidden talent for car repairs? We make an unbeatable team, Ethan."

They hopped back into the car, the engine coughing to life. As they continued their journey, the memory of their comedic and heartwarming climax remained etched in their minds, a testament to their ability to overcome any obstacle together.

With each passing mile, Sarah and Ethan knew that their love was unbreakable, their bond unshakable. The road trip had become more than just a journey—it had become a symbol of their resilience, their ability to find joy even in the face of adversity.

And as they drove into the horizon, their laughter echoing through the rolling hills, Sarah and Ethan were ready to embrace whatever challenges lay ahead, secure in the knowledge that their love story was far from over.

SARAH AND ETHAN HAD journeyed through the ups and downs of their relationship, overcoming obstacles and growing stronger together. Now, as they reached the conclusion of their love story, they found themselves embracing their love and eagerly looking forward to a future filled with laughter and happiness.

One evening, as the sun painted the sky in hues of orange and pink, Sarah and Ethan sat on their porch, sipping mugs of steaming hot chocolate. The air was filled with a sense of contentment and tranquility.

Sarah gazed at Ethan, her heart filled with warmth. "I never imagined we'd come this far, Ethan. From the moment we met, our lives have been intertwined in the most beautiful way."

Ethan smiled, his eyes reflecting the love he felt for Sarah. "Indeed, Sarah. Our journey has been filled with unexpected turns, but I wouldn't change a single moment. Every joy, every challenge has brought us closer."

Sarah reached out and took Ethan's hand, her touch gentle and reassuring. "You've brought so much laughter into my life, Ethan. Your sense of humor and your ability to see the bright side of every situation has taught me the value of finding joy in the little things."

Ethan squeezed Sarah's hand, his voice filled with sincerity. "And you, Sarah, have shown me the true meaning of unconditional love. Your kindness, compassion, and unwavering support have made me a better person."

They sat there in comfortable silence, savoring the warmth of their connection and the promise of a shared future. The laughter that had woven its way through their love story echoed in their hearts, a reminder of the joy they had found in each other.

Sarah broke the silence, a playful glint in her eyes. "You know, Ethan, I can't wait to grow old with you. I can already picture us sitting on this porch, wrinkled and gray, still sharing laughter and making new memories."

Ethan chuckled, his laughter mingling with the fading daylight. "Oh, Sarah, you're stuck with me for life. I promise to be your partner in mischief, your shoulder to lean on, and your eternal source of terrible jokes."

Sarah laughed, her voice filled with affection. "I wouldn't have it any other way, Ethan. Our love is a never-ending adventure, and I can't wait to explore the world and create countless memories with you."

As the night sky enveloped them, Sarah and Ethan held onto each other, their love radiating through the darkness. They knew that their happily ever after was not a destination but a continuous journey, one that they were ready to embark on hand in hand.

And as they looked out into the starry expanse, Sarah and Ethan could almost hear the future calling their names, whispering of laughter, happiness, and a love that would forever unravel the deepest strings of their hearts.

Media Attribution

S ummer time is perfect for sightseeing
Image by gpointstudio[1] on Freepik

About the Author

L ily Enchant is an enigmatic and passionate author known for her captivating romance novels that sweep her readers away. With her flair for heartfelt stories and complicated relationships, Lily Enchant weaves tales that transport the reader into worlds of love, desire and emotional depth.

Lily's writing style is characterized by evocative prose, distinctive character development and a deep understanding of the complexities of love. Her novels explore a wide range of romantic themes, from tender and poignant stories about lovers who get in each other's way, to fiery and passionate encounters that set the pages on fire.

As an author, Lily Enchant believes in the transformative power of love and its ability to touch hearts, heal wounds and inspire personal growth. Her stories delve into the depths of human emotion and capture the essence of vulnerability, resilience and the pursuit of true happiness.

Lily's readers often lose themselves in her enchanting tales and cannot resist the pull of her well-crafted plots and sympathetic characters. Her books have a loyal fan base who eagerly await each new release and enjoy immersing themselves in the enchanting worlds she creates.

With each new novel, Lily Enchant captures hearts and leaves an indelible mark on the romance genre. Her words have the power to inspire hope, ignite passions and remind readers of the beauty that lies within the human heart.

Don't miss out!

Visit the website below and you can sign up to receive emails whenever Lily Enchant publishes a new book. There's no charge and no obligation.

https://books2read.com/r/B-A-BOSFB-VVNAD

BOOKS 2 READ

Connecting independent readers to independent writers.

Did you love *Love and Laughter*? Then you should read *Heartstrings Unraveled*[1] by Lily Enchant!

[2]

"Heartstrings Unraveled" is a captivating romance novel that takes readers on a journey of love, self-discovery, and the pursuit of dreams. Set in a vibrant city renowned for its thriving music scene, the story follows the life of Emma Bennett, a talented violinist struggling to find fulfillment in both her career and personal life.

Emma, the protagonist, possesses an unwavering desire for success and a deep passion for music. However, despite her talent, she feels stuck and unfulfilled, yearning for something more. It is during this time of uncertainty that Emma has a chance encounter with Liam Anderson, an enigmatic and charismatic writer, at a local café. Sparks of attraction

1. https://books2read.com/u/baEp68

2. https://books2read.com/u/baEp68

ignite between them during their brief conversation, leaving both intrigued.

Emma, driven by her musical aspirations, initially hesitates to pursue a relationship with Liam. However, fate intervenes, and they coincidentally meet again at a charity event where Emma is performing. Liam's profound appreciation for Emma's music and his encouragement to pursue her dreams create an unforeseen connection between them. As they spend more time together, their friendship blossoms, and they begin to share their dreams, fears, and personal stories, deepening their emotional connection.

Yet, their path to happiness is not without obstacles. Emma finds it challenging to balance her music career, personal life, and her growing feelings for Liam. Professional setbacks and self-doubt test her determination and commitment, while external pressures, such as disapproval from her family or unexpected circumstances, complicate their relationship.

Through her emotional journey, Emma begins to realize that love and personal fulfillment can coexist with her musical aspirations. Liam becomes her unwavering support and pillar of strength, encouraging her to embrace her authentic self and rediscover her passion for music. As Emma experiences personal growth, she learns to navigate the complexities of her own desires and dreams.

The climax of the story arrives when Emma is faced with a difficult choice between her career and her love for Liam. This pivotal moment leads to an emotional confrontation that becomes a significant turning point in their relationship. Emma must make a decision that will have a profound impact on both her personal and professional life.

The resolution of "Heartstrings Unraveled" follows Emma's journey of finding harmony between her music, love life, and personal happiness. She experiences reconciliation and a deepening of her relationship with Liam. Ultimately, Emma triumphs with a musical performance that represents her growth and newfound balance.

In the conclusion, readers glimpse Emma and Liam's future together, filled with love, support, and shared dreams. Emma realizes that love and pursuing her passion can intertwine, bringing her fulfillment. The closing scene leaves readers with a sense of hope and the belief in the power of love to overcome obstacles and shape one's destiny.

Also by Lily Enchant

Contemporary Romance
Heartstrings Unraveled

Romantic Comedy
Love and Laughter

About the Author

Lily Enchant is an enigmatic and passionate author known for her captivating romance novels that sweep her readers away. With her flair for heartfelt stories and complicated relationships, Lily Enchant weaves tales that transport the reader into worlds of love, desire and emotional depth.

Lily's writing style is characterized by evocative prose, distinctive character development and a deep understanding of the complexities of love. Her novels explore a wide range of romantic themes, from tender and poignant stories about lovers who get in each other's way, to fiery and passionate encounters that set the pages on fire.

As an author, Lily Enchant believes in the transformative power of love and its ability to touch hearts, heal wounds and inspire personal growth. Her stories delve into the depths of human emotion and capture the essence of vulnerability, resilience and the pursuit of true happiness.

Lily's readers often lose themselves in her enchanting tales and cannot resist the pull of her well-crafted plots and sympathetic characters. Her books have a loyal fan base who eagerly await each new release and enjoy immersing themselves in the enchanting worlds she creates.

With each new novel, Lily Enchant captures hearts and leaves an indelible mark on the romance genre. Her words have the power to inspire hope, ignite passions and remind readers of the beauty that lies within the human heart.

About the Publisher

Blissful Romance Books is a haven for lovers of love, a sanctuary where timeless tales of romance find their home. Our mission is simple yet profound: to curate and publish exceptional romance novels that transport readers to worlds brimming with heart-stirring emotions and unforgettable characters.

With an unwavering commitment to quality and an insatiable appetite for evocative storytelling, Blissful Romance Books aims to become a beacon of excellence in the genre. We believe in the power of love to inspire, heal, and transform, and it is this belief that drives us to seek out the most enthralling stories and talented authors to share with our passionate audience.

Milton Keynes UK
Ingram Content Group UK Ltd.
UKHW011116100424
440866UK00001B/24

9 798224 795123